T0000189

VOX
HUMANA

VOX HUMANA

Adebe DeRango-Adem

POEMS

Book*hug Press · Toronto 2022

FIRST EDITION
© 2022 by Adebe DeRango-Adem

ALL RIGHTS RESERVED

No part of this publication may be reproduced or transmitted in any form or
by any means, electronic or mechanical, including photocopying, recording, or
any information storage or retrieval system, without permission in writing from
the publisher.

Library and Archives Canada Cataloguing in Publication

Title: Vox humana / Adebe DeRango-Adem.
Names: DeRango-Adem, Adebe, author.
Description: Poems.
Identifiers: Canadiana (print) 20220210101 | Canadiana (ebook) 20220210136
ISBN 9781771667845 (softcover)
ISBN 9781771667869 (PDF)
ISBN 9781771667852 (EPUB)
Classification: LCC PS8607.E7145 V69 2022 | DDC C811/.6—dc23

The production of this book was made possible through the generous assistance of
the Canada Council for the Arts and the Ontario Arts Council. Book*hug Press also
acknowledges the support of the Government of Canada through the Canada Book
Fund and the Government of Ontario through the Ontario Book Publishing Tax Credit
and the Ontario Book Fund.

Book*hug Press acknowledges that the land on which we operate is the traditional
territory of many nations, including the Mississaugas of the Credit, the Anishnabeg,
the Chippewa, the Haudenosaunee, and the Wendat peoples. We recognize the
enduring presence of many diverse First Nations, Inuit, and Métis peoples and are
grateful for the opportunity to meet, work, and learn on this territory.

Book*hug Press

CONTENTS

FUGUE I
VOX INFIRMI / AMOR 18
VOX APSENS / ANASTASIS 19
VOX MUTO / VERITAS 20
VOX PIUS / CLARUS 23
VOX AUXILIUM / NOCIVIS 28
VOX LUDO / LIGNUM 30
VOX VIVUS / TREMOLO 33
VOX ARDENS / FERVENS 35
VOX REFUGIUM 37
VOX TELUM / MEMORIAM 39
VOX GRAVIS / PHANTASMA 40
VOX VORTO / VINDICTA 42
VOX NEBULA / FABULAR 43

FUGUE II
VOX CONSONE / NAVITAS 49
VOX GENUS / PROVECTUS 51
VOX SENTIO / FIDELITAS 53
VOX LINGUA / MALEDICTUM 59
VOX ASTRA / ASTERISK 62
VOX CORDIA / CANTUS 66

FUGUE III
VOX AMPLIO / ANTIPHONA 69
VOX SALVO / EXSOLVO 72
VOX PULMONES / PERCUSSIO 79
VOX NOX 83
VOX INFELIX / AGNOSIS 85
VOX EXEMPLUM 90

for the silenced & clairaudient amongst us

As all the Heavens were a Bell,
And Being, but an Ear,
And I, and Silence, some strange Race
Wrecked, solitary, here –
—Emily Dickinson ("I felt a Funeral, in my Brain")

if you wd have me speak
you must learn the tongue of my dead & loved ones
i have been left behind
a survivor
holdin out for more
—Ntozake Shange ("for my dead & loved ones")

vox vōcis, f. (connected with *voco*), a *voice, cry, call.*
  (1) of things, *sound, tone;*
  (2) *a thing said with the voice, a saying, utterance,*
    formula, magic incantation.[1]

FUGUE I

inspire (v.)

mid-14c., *enspiren*, "to fill (the mind, heart, etc., with grace, etc.)"; also "to prompt or induce (someone to do something)," from Old French *enspirer* (13c.), from Latin *inspirare* "blow into, breathe upon," figuratively "inspire, excite, inflame," from *in-* "in" (from PIE root **en* "in") + *spirare* "to breathe" (see spirit (n.)). The Latin word was used as a loan-translation of Greek *pnein* in the Bible. General sense of "influence or animate with an idea or purpose" is from late 14c. Also sometimes used in literal sense in Middle English. Related: Inspires; inspiring.

TO BUILD OUT OF NECESSITY   out of this   *hissssssssss*

grrrr-gle   (stifled—   / muffled)

         cry   for a worthier world

    for a body   tenacious   & not so

   out of breath

      to build   out of survival's ruins.   a   *lingua*

       a *langue*   "in other words"

       a long line

       of echoes   / lineages

         fighting for

           auricular coherence

     & yet a type of peace when you

        hear   that   unmistakable

      key / of   variegated & unenglish sounds

        received in the ears   as   jewels

        / small prisms   abstracted

  from the heavy

     peninsulas

we slipped   / from

       we didn't land

       to craft some humdrum idiom

       from some *ho-hum* lips

   this is / a script

       a   will   to   reach   chest-first

     into the wise   voluminous

       nest of glimmering

verbs / to will   the word

                per word

         story of

             what comes next

but first to recant

what preceded

      what was lost

        / be(come) witness

          to a new metrics

               that renews

        &   renames   you

      says you

   matter says   to   you   on the down lo of yo   self-
self   / lo

        & behold

        even when you   are
        forcedintothemarginalia
    / you are building yourself

                      an exit
         out of the domain of   unsaid
     things

     / to   declare &   round
    them
up   one by one

     until they form
     a makeshift drum
/ *beating beating*   in the jewel
   of your ear

familiar   yet emergent

       present
               / yet   yet

     (to go bold into the   / yet to be
             heard of

     is   the   only   home

            I've known)

VOX INFIRMI / AMOR

WE WERE NOT MADE SO FRAGILE / how else to explain
our ability to escape / wars escape self escape self-war /
we were not made so meek / how else to carry the heaviness
of ages in each / anguished beat of the blood / how else to perform
the necessary rupture / heed to the need to retrieve a landing
/ embroider our allies carefully into the fabrics / of what we are
& trust few with the tools in our arsenal of muses / how else
to be but to let ourselves be changed without notice
let ourselves notice each change of heart / for where the heart
breaks a new line oft begins

VOX APSENS / ANASTASIS

LISTEN   UP   I HEARD   THE   DEAD   CAN TALK   &   looks   like
they have a lot to say / *ehhhhhhhh* / a sound between a(h) and e(h) /
nesyamun[2] the true of voice / ancient   priest & chanter of egypt
thanks be to 3-D for a way to print / these BC phonics these pharaonic
vocal tracts   into tracks so fresh / can't touch this sphinx that sits
at my larynx / biggest cool cat of all   coming at you   from the OG
mantra   /   by which   you   speak   the   name   of the dead
& they live   again / but does pronunciation count / which syllables
        get counted   / can you   mispronounce a death / am I cursed
                                       to   be   anon   /   a   wind-
gone insignia at my wake / whatever
happens tell them not to underestimate
        the energy of   the dead or forget the affluence of
            being alive   trying I am trying
            with words   to   be   a   kind mirror
        spinning my tale to the decibels   of my own joy / to exhume
                               each & every   mummified
                                 voice
    I   free them all   into the future
                               to chant   their golden   vicissitudes
            &   dance   in / audible   shapes
& what's in a name   but a calibration always   incomplete
        what's a name   but a vow   a root

VOX MUTO / VERITAS

... All we have to give each other is
Our breath, our darkness breathing
Life into the dying lungs of the night...
            —Gwendolyn MacEwen (from "Marino Marini's Horses & Riders")

once upon a time I thought   my body a sound
            thought   my body   a sound
                  thing
                        but illness made it L O U D
                              & clear that it was time to
                  learn how to die
in secret
            so I hid   my heaving
            amid the orchestra   of cities
                                    not knowing how disease
                              makes   frames   of reference
                              change
                                    makes you lose
                                          (the   face
                                    you worked
                                    hard to save)
      passing through
                  taking nothing

      into the subtle scrawl
            of unexceptional days

                                    / call it
                                    a requiem for all
                              my languages /

inclasstheyteach
"everyutteranceindialoguewithother
utterances"

        (says who)   what I learned   is silence is

                                               a removal

                    / silence can   move you

          to aggravate the wound
       even at the risk
   of more silencing

whatmattersisthatyourespond
towhathesaidshesaidtheysaid

        (who said)   in truth I'd rather
they don't want   talk about
                        the hydrauli

                / earliest pipe organ from north
    africa
              / how water was used as wind
                       (for sound)

           / how was it these primordial organs
       were shipped
             'cross the waters to
               (an allegory)

  europe   / how what
     drowns you

          can also carry you   depending
          how careful you cross

(with elegies in tow)

                      into that boundless   blue
                        much better this voice /

                I

                belong to no one

my true nature
/ the map

of my anatomy

          hegira

                (without   end)

VOX PIUS / CLARUS

PSYCHO-BABBLE TO WHOM in these rooms with zero books & only
gloomy medicated stares   is all I'm saying / say I'm   here because my
yelling professors couldn't understand / having   a   hull   a   hollow
        instead of a throat   instead of a voice   a   clashing of phantom
                                                                    bells / or
were they shells / orixa   is this / the right shore / ximaya
            what   seaward prayer
        shall I use to get home   / they put me in this room
                                        & left my self   outside
is this where I stop pretending I can breathe   underwater / I came
with dreams of a salvador shore / a want   to remove myself
from stolen land but I am / locked up
& on my birthday no less /   I came ready
                                    to die can't recall how I
                              arrived
/ surmised gravity this long   long enough
            to eclipse
                        my substantive self / remember only
                              surrendering
            my keys & identities   at the door

/ impatient first time in the city of firsts:
            first hospital penitentiary asylum zoo
/ first city that asked you to disrobe from all
            scholastic composure   / you the same now

as that girl who keeps getting thrown

in the quiet
room / everyone knows
when you go in there   you leave

your   self
behind
come out a faint light

a wail
/ every body so busy with agonies   no one

hears

my ivory   tower tales   / knows how it all   went down

hear this—
in this city of firsts   foremost you are Black
& when the white
coats come
you will be   even blacker
/ they don't care
how beautiful you are
or if you stand tall or play
the pipe organ with your
hands & feet

it's lunchtime

& your new friend the blind ex-con
wheels himself into the kitchen

he's got perfect hearing   but feels nothing
in his legs   lost his sight
after trying to kill himself
after trying to kill someone
/ you hand him the last apple

drink because you know it's his favourite

                                   then it's time for the grown-ups
                    to shuffle their wounds
                    back down the bismol halls

              get by by feeling   as little as possible
              / if you get through this

                          you promise
      to invent a better word for desire
            one that conveys how   to accept
                  only   the   glorious   into your
          mouth

        when you get out
          you'll summon back   your centre

              develop a taste for water
    start taking notice of

           the sky
                  bird by
        bird

but first   you must get to the bottom of it until   the din

                that runs red   in your ears runs

           out

      & you are able to scatter   your   voice
                 in a thousand
               directions & far away
        enough from the law

& you may become   home
                              sick   in a hundred directions
to row gently up   this stream of blood
            this rush of waves
            this din runs red in the ears

    at least   meds beds & being fed by   beautiful Black
nurses from north   philly to the six is this what   success looks
like or what myspeechslurs cuz drugsmakemesee

    make   me   clean white bright   more quiet than I remember
I am with alogia³   & nowIam a logos   a logic without speech
    I tell them it's pre-existing thispoverty
        ofspeechofwords
                        I keep telling them
                              always telling them
                                      about loss
    tellthemaboutthis loss   thislossthis
        povertymypoverty my loss mywordsmy
            lossthislack mywords mylack my

26

on a scale of one to ten what is your pain level is it manageable like a one or
emergency like a ten if you been broken open how many times would you say
have you experienced any bouts of freedom what kind of noises are you hearing
are the instructions coming from one or more voices have you ever experienced
the feeling that you're not real or do you bounce from dusk to duskier real quick
do you ever feel like there's no justice do you ever feel like a cartoon or like what's
real cannot stay for how long have you been experiencing trouble sleeping how
long do you think your troubles have been about your date of birth o daughter of
immigrants have you ever run away from home we will run some tests do you
know where you are now have you any issues with your teeth being broken have
you ever run away from tests or experienced trouble at home have you ever not
had a home how did you crack so many teeth what are your thoughts about dusk
do you ever feel like an emergency is your hearing real do you need a hearing on
a scale from one to ten how painful is justice how long have you been broken by
experience do you have any problems with speech

VOX AUXILIUM / NOCIVIS

BEST   BE   MOVED   BY   MY   WORDS

      the way they   miscegenate   sound   into moon
                               energy
                                      tides   reach
     as   text   reach
                       that shore
a way
       to honour
those   gone aboard   the night train

     shooby-doo   *choo-choo* / next stop rosetta
                        station followed   by
                                      bessie
                 then etta / where you better
         transfer to line miles
                        or louis or
                 dizzy
   bless us with your
   dizzying
      intervals / uncanny construction

of cries   within cries   for five years I lived

down the street / from billie   on lombard
   in the city of
     brotherly love
              / chasing her moans

never knowing the doctors refused her   last request
for a candy
/ denied her mouth

PEACEBEUPONTHEM

who left her a wanted woman / woman in want
& wild on her death
bed

PEACEWILLNOTCOME

now that my tongue is a knife
never drawing blood
always ready
to kill

from   *the*   *womb*   *to*   *the*   *tomb*   *I*   *be*   *running*

my   *mouth*   *till*   *nobody*   *unsafe*   *nobody*

unsound

VOX LUDO / LIGNUM

WHITE   PEOPLE   STAGE   A   DIE-IN / inside bright chalk
outlines / you played us all your life / & now you play on our death
/ you make it so   we have to imagine you / dead to keep ourselves
alive   / tho' we know you can't die / like us you can kneel
but *how low can you go*   / I can hardly   bear
going back / to central park   I'm afraid of the timbre of
trees *shiver*   *me   timbers*
once said the ships / who saw   the storm coming
timberrrrrr   we say as   the tree   falls down
then the sound
of the splitting   wood   beams   of   the   hull
exposed   explode into   a   range of
subharmonic pieces of course
when the bough breaks no tone
can contain all the   textures /
subordinate sounds so   when you hear someone
describing a sound as "bright" or   "dark" what they mean is
two sounds can have   the   amplitude
the same structure   / pitch
same loudness but why do only light
sounds get to sustain their   timbre
                        what
matters   is to grow
almost anything you need both
light & shade

        they go so well together   strange   fruit
              of the same tree

                            which is just to say

this world is strange &

crawling   with

vampires who know
/ the neck is best like
                                                            police

        like a country's

whose lifeblood depends upon
            the red
                        of Black sorrow

                    staining the river-
                    water

                beside the white
                ~~cosplayers~~ cause players

how the steady soft crescendo of time turns talking to yourself necessary to
document the
    days monday I am here & like the street   *childless & the wind*

    is something you can hear   *tuesday's vesper*
            gives way to wednesday's living   *song but I was a friday*

child   full of loving   &giving   & I grew to love chasing

                              the black sequin dresses of cities

           in the

                night   to let men chase me in

               whorls

                    let them think how curious I am

      happier

          than ever alone   with my circuitry

               my mind

                  a radiant smear

at best a span of shadow-work

               record of small delinquencies

      did I leave enough

              aspects of my is-ness in the phonic

ether did I speak   truth

especially where unwelcome   tell me

           how best to translate these

       indigo moods

VOX VIVUS / TREMOLO

CURSUS   SOLITUS   NATURAE!   give   your   trembling
eyelids to the mortal day   let the flaming   caravan
        stay hungry   give in only   to   the   harrowing
hours   when they come   prepared
           to   instruct   with   quiet

        evidence   of what makes us crucial
against the   faceless machinery
                  inherited strata   of   days

                we survive with the residue
        of what remains of
the corporeal in
        a world where you can
        3-D   print a gun

we have all the dimensions we need
        when music moves   through our physics

                even easier ways to bend a
        Black body
into negative space

    no matter
        I was told BLM but how
can I matter
        until I   take   up   space
        on   earth

when billions blasted up to space
for   kicks   as

      one miniature step of   *humanus*

      away families' faces crumple
      facing eviction watching

their home fold   in 2-D

VOX ARDENS / FERVENS

I AM IN RAHIM'S NISSAN & ON THE RADIO / ariana is squealing God / is a woman & suddenly / all the trees emerge cathedral / an aria of voices lifted & / with every branch a voice / I think of the bruised & putrefying / orb of paradiso / half-eaten in the prehistoric sun / what knowledge trickled into / the veins of the vast foliage / what became of the blemished organisms / the flora that fell from the heavens & into / a state of disarray / what to say to my fallen / ones who enriched this soil / with their bones at this / point my reflection / bends into an agony & this pop song has me thinking about graveyards though graver things have muddied my mind / like the man[4] who set himself aflame / what ballad did he last of his body / & will its scattering cup had runneth / over too soon extinguish / his face himself from the noise white of the white of the white walk calmly & alight until the surprise

on the grounds / of the manicured park / listen to before striking / the match all / over the nation's capital / what what thirst / had forced him to instead of last words / subtract of tourists & the blinding house & by way of resolve of death entering the

body's rooms its chambers of fatherbrothersonwhatever the masquerade now reducing   to an assemblage of flames his red usa shirt   smouldering   what   to   make   of   a   grown   man burnt   to   shape   a   shape   drummmmmed back   through   time   like   he's   done this   before   did   he   last   cry   out   for   God   or the   mother   of   God   or   his   mother   womb *"...God is a wom—"*

by this time the song is over
& we are turning onto my street / I cannot be sure how
imagination will serve me now or if I am worthy of serving myself
of arriving at the place where fire becomes a last solace / final plea
we talk about superheroes but imagine being so
willing to take a penultimate huff
& go out
a small velocity

to teach by turning oneself all

the way back
into a whirl of
atoms

VOX REFUGIUM

BY ALL HISTORICAL / logic my phenotype should have disappeared /
should not have been / by now yet here I was / is / am / & before poetry
I wanted / to be a spy / perhaps they are the same / wanting to melt
into / the psychology of things / thirty years ago today / basquiat died
& here I am   watching white nationalists / gather in the capital
           / it is enough

                                        to make anyone   want to put down
                         brushpenself / pick up   gunbombdrink / best
               case I drown out the voice that says
                    to disappear / if I am still here
I must be

                         a spy   my only trace   the sand-

steps of a shell   it appears   my second sight
                                               has served me well

TRUTH BE (A) TOLD (thing) / wherever I am / beached   is where I belong / my only map   a   parameter / of scars   like crusoe's numbered days   an algebraic / attempt   to live & relay how / in meeting the other / we   are   opened   to   the   foreign   self / the   hovering   birthright we   have   built   by   /   perfecting   the   sound   of   the   sea-bound tongue / the song that relays / the cusp & cull of history's attempt / to make from the shipwrecks / of chance an unbroken wave / but it knows   how voice goes / & how it   came created / cannot be   destroyed / dear   time   strange   chariot / of   beauty lead   us   into / our   wounds   with   thanksgiving / be   never   still my   itinerant   heart

VOX TELUM / MEMORIAM

GREAT FOREST CHORUS OF SCREAMS / composition in a key
of a tree reluctant to give life / the wood that relays
decay so discreetly / you would have to listen
with your eyes   the sound of silence you see / is a real
thing in the shape of a valley   omega of murmurs
of mostly children / in these alpine lines   the howl of a hungry jaw
the sharp teeth that so easily slide into place   like a hyena's
    / & into a woman's life I walk with those with lives left behind

/ last time I came to walk   the black oak
         savannah commonly known
         as high park   I recalled my maternal
last name & how it means   scythe or sickle
in reference to   the crescent shape of the mother-

land I am named after something sharp
         like a tool to hurt or to   harvest

      I am named   after mothers
        who watched their
        lesions wane &   wax
         & wane

VOX GRAVIS / PHANTASMA

ONLY IN DREAMSCAPES NOW DO YOU DROP / into my body's
dredges like the time you stood / over the niagara & past
the barricades & smiling / you wanted me to snap
your photo   *I should have / known*
then not to speak to or of   *the   black   sea*
your childhood / or try & temper   *the   cold   steel*
that face   *I tried in vain with poesy*
to deduce who hurt you   *along the helices*
of your biology / was it   *the combined weight of your country's*
tragic tales of   *derailed   love*
or that you'd never / take in or to the thick   *discourse of dreams...*
in dream I carry you home though /
    do not spend the night   *drinking*
in your strange   *&   hysterical   beauty*
in dream I have the courage
        to tell you   *as relic I kept an x-ray*
of your lungs / part of the grad school
        requirements for foreigners
/ I imagine them even clearer   *now   you   are   free*
from my many opaque
                        attributes   *& will no longer hear me*
trying to disappear   *into the night's chimes*
guess what I'm still here   *if only you'd had the eyes to*

        see me in my fullness .
                        with   *if only the ears to*
                                                hear

how well I really do

     in the silence

& you weren't just a wolf

    all those years

VOX VORTO / VINDICTA

NOT   *RRRRRREVOLUCIÓN* /   but   perejil /   *perejil* /, parsley was the word / on the block / that had meant / all the difference / 'twixt life & death / for the Black of la dominicana[5] / unable to roll their r's / *perejil* / was the glossal test / roll your tongue or die / I consider my own clefted / tongue & how I would have been / denied a less pedestrian ending / more worthy last word / how I would have tried & tried / for my life to say / the cursed word / so in the name of each tongue-tied early ancestor / I   give   you   what   air / left   of   my   lungs

may it be the aperture   your memory needs / the way pallets[6]
must yield to the depression   of keys to reach / the cascading
intervals / it breathes & what goes down   / comes   up   arranged
like flowers   on   the   verge   of
unrehearsed   rupture / a bloom
naming what was   lost

VOX NEBULA / FABULAR

WE IMAGINED OURSELVES TO BE TENNESSEE / williams's
ladies of the fog / speeding down highway 30 / past the cemeteries
& trailer parks / wondering how people just go about living / how men
go about forgetting / my vertebrae soften each time I am asked
/ to consider the maladies of others / & all the sad people I tried & tried to
love / but now all we need is a spark / a match to light the way / back
to that elliptical range of dreams / I am telling you a thing can heal
without causing pain / if it hurts / try again & before / you know it the
notes / will begin mounting from your mouth / & you will be mouthing /
words of worship   in a tongue outside your tongue

IN   AN   EVEN   EARLIER   LIFE   /   you   may   have   been / a   semiprecious   stone   /   colombina   mulatta   /   ptolemaic   bone   / old   church   bell   or   bell   hop   /   songstress   in   a   moonlit room   /   or   were   you   the   song   /   the   trespassing tune   wailing   /   into   midnight's   &   heaven's   largesse or   something   equally   vexing   /   &   hurling   with   wishes beautiful   &   Black   &   holy   holy

... *CHECK   CHECK   one   two   CHECK   check   one*
two check check three   check third   check vision check third   eye
looks   good   check   light   check   sound   we   resound   check   it

we   see   so   clear   can't   won't   stop   for   death

what   say   you

of   this   brief

rugged   prelude

to infinity

[la la la la   we say
to pretend we're not listening
but   the   hearing
has   already   begun]

FUGUE II

conspire (v.)

late 14c., "aspire or plan maliciously," from Old French *conspirer* (14c.), from Latin *conspirare* "to agree, unite, plot," literally "to breathe together," from *com* "with, together" + *spirare* "to breathe."

VOX CONSONE / NAVITAS

HEAR   ME   OUT   /   DEAR   BREAD   OF   LIFE
pantry on carnegie   ave / dear botanical   gardens   /
thing of curatorial beauty   I can try & tune   out   the
loud swirling   of trees / green as money   / that beautify the
broken   streets / try & drown   out the sound of
the vacant   row homes empty abodes / of dead millionaires
          with songs   on the radio / but when that song   about   the
rains   in africa   comes on / I begin   dreaming of   axum
nubia / how we reigned   / in reality I am facing lake erie
          & the marina / where two Black men   in thick   camouflage
coats fish & talk   about God   /   in reality they are likely
/ conversing in murmurs / grunts   in veteran speak / & by this time
it is raining   ever   so   slightly   on   euclid   /   &   I   pass
two more elderly   men / with soft branches   for   a   body
/ & in an abstract maternal   gesture /   as if to   say   sorry
for the war   that conscripted you   so as to   script your life
/ into a theatre of pain

(or is it / the pain we share / I see /
in which I am / your understudy)

          / a production in which you are known for
          your famous last lines

(or do we need / to switch up
that storyline)

          / including the one that "philanthropy"
          wasn't   the   result   of   "giving"
                    Black people   hell

& still we gave

you   our children
                    who became your
mistresses
even gave you our   musics

let you mimic our medicinal   blues

what   say   you   amiri
                    I   can   hear   you

        sonia   hear   you   hughes

is it because we made you that you don't want us because
you
            need us   like sight

                needs darkness   to   make   sense
                            of   light

VOX GENUS / PROVECTUS

THESE   LINES   BE   A   LONG   TIME COMING FOR THESE
                                       lines   come   from   far
          away & long   ago
                                    people with a taste
                                       for a full   self   &   dark
                                       fascinating
          rhythms   of   yore
                                                        forecasts
               auricular-oracular
                    lore in lines long   logged

                         with messages
                                                  singeing

               on the tongue of a great-great-
          uncle   oracle   for the people
                                        a   people   singing

                                                  on   the   mountain
                              assigning axumite   knowledge
     & my father who had no father
                    before he was my father
     belonged   to this people
               who kept moving
          on fascists & missionaries
                    who kept stepping

out of line

a lineage of hands

hands baked in sun

tasked with carving a medieval

church beneath rock

the country

I am *reeeeeally* from

is a record

I play back

to the age of wizards by trade

to come from   my country

is to arrive   at the beginning of

multitudes

these pages

once   upon   a   tree

read best by

listening

to   the   rhizomes beneath

a   ruckus network

of howls

VOX SENTIO / FIDELITAS

dear reader I know you know

        your   ABCDEFGs   but do you know

   your   ADCs   your   after-
                                    death

                communications

spontaneous encounters

            with the deceased

A   is for   burning

            amazon as in   B for brasil

   not bezos whose bank

                account   be on fire as we   C for

         click click add to cart   but C stands for climate

change   *see*   *I see no changes*   see only
                                    chokehold

                chaff   history a crystal

    blood   diamond

D for   dendrology   for   did you know
    a monoculture   forest has species
                    of tree where if one is destroyed

   the others   close by   close themselves up   curl

their leaves to   commune   injury   limn the alarm

                                   but a person is not a tree if you
                         hack us we do not return we lumber
day in day out
            D is for
                  distress signal

                                             sometimes   racism so thick
        I can't see the forest for   the trees

       E is for example if one person of colour   dies   don't   we   all
lose   oxygen

                           // this is not a poem but smoke signal //

                                   can't see my way over
        the slate of the sky   the   river
                                          & through   the wood

on the way to   grandma's house
                         by   the   humber   where   I'd
                                          pined
                  for a boy named   neil johnson
                                          for seven years
            'til we were twelve hoping

                      he'd pick   me for the dance

        & he did   & finally kissed me   in the arboreal

lagoon with a lizard   tongue   neil you here neil can you hear I
                    know you loved me
          even the years I danced   alone

vicki said   she ran into you   on queen   west
                          along the stretch
              not taken over by hip-capitalists
                                          & that you were
                          homeless now   do   you
                    remember how
              popular you were
                                      I remember

you trying to suck a du maurier from a straw   & speak a thick

                                        french accent
                through your perfect teeth
            but you choked
                          on the smoke

                                                // this poem smoke //

            coughing & laughing
                                        trying 'til you
                                            got it   right
    not all of us get it right
                    the first time   I get it

                          that shelters are not always   a place

                                  to exhale   that exhaling
                is a difficult art
                          in a surveilled space

                  & no room   to dance
    like we did   to   *usher   usher   usher usher*

making the other girls   jelly
                    did you keep your celebrity
        smile   how did you manage

                                        to make it through the
                                night after night after night after
                                night after night after night after
                                night after night

                        & what is   love
                                is it
        a guarantee we won't   fissure

        listen if you see me
                            I hope you cuss me
                        in patois
            like you used to   & I will look for you

    please don't sneer   if I find you
                        & can't speak   just come with jazz
    hands flailing
                    with money & money

    don't judge if it's not enough
            to make   you feel rich like you made
                        me   but if I
                find you   best believe in what my
                            hands can do   'nuff talk
                            I will weave
                                        our palms
            together   so you never leave
                                        will you
    have this dance

56

I   hear   your   laugh   like   yesterday

&   *TO   BE   HEARD   IS   TO   BE*
TRULY   LOVED
&   to   be   loved   is   to   have
each   layer   of   you   you   are
willing   to   unfold   be   listened   to
          poems
                    a   calling   but   poems
                                        too   a call
                    to unfold & uncover
          the bodies
               we've left behind

for each time a Black body falls   &   I   am not   there   to   hear   it
I   feel   it

                              the   way   a   capital-r   romantic   feels
               them   *intimations of*
                         immortality

                                             every death
               I   hear   a   throwback

                                        for every death
          throws   me   back
to   the   brute   vernal
          equinox   brute   vernacular
at   the   root
          of   this   dub   this   *is a throwback*

          I   hear   you   I   hear   all

               the   vowels   *a tide lifting*

a   heralding

             in   my   throat

             &   I   know   *I am loved*

                          you are loved

VOX LINGUA / MALEDICTUM

a sailor's farewell[7]

O COMMONWEALTH—! I HEX your gilded lexicons—! I spook
the master's language   I see how   texts
     turn white & whiter   foam

          the colour of dissolve

               pages stained   cannot be ocean-
washed   the master stained the language   strained it
                    of colour   white pages
                              over the oral

          tradition   typographical script
               less cryptic
than a sound   you can echo into a body   of work
                                        that does the work
                    of pulling a body   out of water

     english   I have no name
                         in your body
                              though I take your nation-
                         language   into my mouth   every day
          to commune
this is the way & the life   my nucleo-
                         tides
                              return the unsaid

an ultra sound   reveals an unsound   lack
                              a   burst

          of code   deciphered only by bodies
          that know that lyric domain of   *watch me whip & watch me*

                    unchain these chains
            I fight for any child who becomes
    air
                whose language has no fighting
        chance
                                we are breathing them in
even now
                    what would you say   if I told you
        every word
                is a shared somatic thing
                an unmerciful thing
                    you can't unsee or unfeel
        once you've gone into that bygone   music

        see here I go again   feeling my way through
                        by   way   of   aretha's   score   nina's   odes
voices arranged   in a field of all-blue sounds   all   blues
sounds thick as fog   until   I   am   no   longer
                seeing   just spinning   searching for
    an exit   that never comes
                        & so you take in the disquiet that speaks
            loud to the lonely
                    who learn to repurpose desire
        this too is a   code
                        but what to do with this "breaking
                        news"   of mass graves
        'neath   the beloved green   country club in
tallahassee
                    so soon after they found
            the ones in tulsa   then the babies
                    in   tk'emlúps
                            the place where the rivers
                        meet
        what you   know about a river anyway

what you know about the black magic of

what you really know about white supremacy

ooo canada you & hey-hey usa too

need a hearing

was either of you listening
when they said a plague
on both your
houses
there shall be
no more

sleek iridescent
poems unless they have found grace in
the guttural

landscape the treble of a body
out of words but to gut the way I speak

you have to unfurl in reverse my hand
back into a fist
a bare-boned (-knuckled)
music hovering
inward
& on the rise
like a fog

ascending
over a sleepy town
like a
question

VOX ASTRA / ASTERISK

SOMEWHERE IN THE WILD WEST OF THE WWW

I read *"eskimo" nebula* &
"siamese" twins galaxy

are out

& lynching is back in as in

I must be time-

travelling

is it time

to holla at another

cosmos

the gravitational pull

will the dead

be raised

against their will

but where

do violent words go

to die   & why

do mine feel

like small

scratched records

were they not listening the

first time

asterisk[8]—I risk

all* for you   for you**

I*** risk   all of me

I throw myself   *ad astra*

if you frisk   me

you'll find

a pocket full   of

stars

in the king james

  it means something marginal / sub-
  scripture

in the ambulance

  that $1,000 ride on the star of life
  / rod of asclepius that says

                    death lives here

on the telephone

        left of zero

on an ad

      the fine print

                  is it emphasis   or
              censorship   is   peace
                          another   name
for war

                  for wavering   in   the   strange

                        celestial

        arrangement   metaphorically   speaking is metaphor
another name for

                  stay with me now
        or
                  there must be more than this

I took to poems   as a caul (call)

                                                    risky act of

          morphogenesis

                    I took   beauty

          tips

from the infusoria
                    who live

                                                    in the waters
                                        below

    look how they dance
                    without skin
          or bones or nails or   blood
                              to   an invisible
                                        music

VOX CORDIA / CANTUS

*dear   rhythmic   throbs   of this   corda lingua / wretched   heart
what use do laws / & principles have in matters of a heart / that thrives & speaks
in riveting chords / over time we learn   to tame / woe's wilderness
withstand / the wretched crossfire if for nothing / but to love again is it love or woe
/ that makes me thrive on rhythms / without law is it useful to withstand / being
leftwretched&hangingon/anuntamedlastchordhowtotame/theheart'swilderness
when / it is a wretch on principle / can I love this wilderness can   I thrive
on wildfire / must I adhere to woe what is / left if nothing but to withstand to the end
/ even if we end up loving useless laws / or are all laws a wilderness / what use are
wretched principles or a wilderness on fire / what's the use of taming a wildfire heart
/ how to   use chords instead of fire / even in the wretched key of woe
why love with wildfire again as if to withstand / can I love without withstanding
can I love without adhering / to nothing should I love notwithstanding / even when the
fire turns useless should I adhere / on principle to the lingua of my heart / in my heart
a wilderness   of   chords   on   fire*

FUGUE III

something is transpiring[9]

becoming known

VOX AMPLIO / ANTIPHONA

the oft-quieted inner voice

how can I write   this   poem when
                    the   poem   has never stopped being
            written
                                    will not stop
        the police   because this poem is not a fist
                    (though it may appear in my fist)
                    nor opposed to opposing   this poem
                                    was written
                    by my fist relaying the gore   a poem
                    was written long before we'd   forgotten
                                    all

            convenient   theories
of otherness   of the others who were opposed
    & stopped
                            I cannot place the year
                    this poem was written in 1812
                        I need   more time   to write
this poem

    & now I can't sleep   staying up
                into the grotesque   hours
thinking about   colonial

    violence   can't get

washington's dentures   out of my head
hurts, styll
      how did he sleep   beside
that small coliseum of teeth
each one   pulled
from a slave & sold to him for less
        than a shilling each   talk about bone-
              chilling
  how awful to eat
      with a full set of lies

              to have to swallow your words
    with   mineral   traces of the slain

  pssst
       I piss
on your parole   I   will not use an "indoor voice"

        can't speak
        to your linguistic
    system
ecclesiastic
    pipeline   parabola   your parole

  must write as antagonist to pathogen

    must write against
even if my words get turned against me

    must go on to tell them
it's more lesson
        learned

                                    say   self-
                                       taught   from

say   (you are)   your   own   material
say   you've   endured   the   obscure

                                    panorama   of   never   being
          sound

               asleep
     never   knowing what the sound of

          safe & sound   might be
                                       knowing   them   only
                                       as words

VOX SALVO / EXSOLVO

a hymn for the hereafter world in two voices

THIS / THESE   *a revelations / in*

                                                              real
            time

    humana / humanus (of the earth) / *humando*

(burying) revolution / *revolvere* (roll back)

                                    / no progress without
                an unveiling

    of the eye / apocalypsis (revelation)

                    to reveal   *by means of*

                being ready to evolve
                through removal after removal

                    / to reveal
                                    the veil as being

/ where   there is a loss   of
                                    a full life

the   excess   effluvia   *becomes*

                                                    a full revolution
                         up
from the ground(s)
                                                      dʰéǵʰōm[10]

    (we do the two-step forward
/ one-step back)
                    on what grounds do you want me

                        on the   ground
        I come armed
                    with   poems of   Black joy

                            though joy   ain't a word

    that slips so easily off   *my tongue*
                                              for now I need
                            my hands

        to pull out all the stops[11]

    one by one
                    we come   *undone*

                    we go   *all   out*

                    ranks at the ready &   *eyes*

all-consumed by not an   -un but an
                                            all-seeing

                                                          73

sorrow but
anguish thank goodness
a coy clairvoyant

an eye-clearing

uprising—

is it a bird is it a plane

/ no the sky is

falling   no   breaking or maybe   *opening*

the heat

a remembering

of all the things

we thought we never had   *to see*

in this life is   air

quality control   is   *all the*
earth

rumbling

dum   spiro   spero!
dum   tacent   clamant!

if I am supposed to be blessed
just to be alive then why am I

always saying farewell
                    (in)to my mind
                                        letting   the   mutiny

            build   slow
              &   sweetly   *in   my   bones*

                                                / into the minutiae

                of last year's haunted
summer
                    soundtrack   strange   *record of brutal sounds*

        Blacks like me dropping
              like tracks
                                            RRRRRRRIOT-sounds

                                        quickening   into   the
                            soundwaves   of

        months   years   the record's
              skipping again

we still   fighting   for the brief solace
              of an intelligible life
                            isn't it enough I confined my mouth to
              the queen's
english   like cpr   & yet I could die
                            birdwatching

or buying candy to console my teenage spirit

in the stifling

air   almost

seems safer to get gone

turn back into the   nothingness

I came from

but each time   *we   say   their   names*

a resonance is born

& bound   *to survive*

into the sheen

of the day

like how the water

is getting   cleaner

in any   case

the   way   death

clarifies things

as night   accumulates   we   like   to   forget

        our roots

               the   nebulous umbilicus

    of an identity made from   trespassing

  having no words

            as in too many words

                  too   much

       weight

  carried in the   constant

running   &   noise   best I run

     out

      of words

          so   I don't run my

      mouth

[too late
you gone know this mouth now
you echolocate me but not for long]

now you see me now you don't

see my blackness you don't

see me now / my blackness

see my blackness / don't see

you as me / my blackness do

you see how my blackness

is a now

VOX PULMONES / PERCUSSIO

lord you are loved but   lo

do you
behold

the non-
& anon   voices

fathoms below can you fathom   father

that we care about space
more than people   lord

at sky
forgive me   if I look up

but   do
not

see you   just
see climate
change   &
ask

compulsively to send me a man

who knows
why the canary
sings

                in the mine

       or a daughter

        immaculate

   like you did your mama

okay fine so I see you

               sometimes   in coral
       skies

           reminding us of   the
         dying
               like snowfall in
           april

    hear you in   jimi joni their
electric

psalms

              transfiguring

     configuring in me

       a brief suspension from   my disbelief

a suspension
                  in time
   a moment of   solace

           for not being killed

    save us o merciful lord   my   father   watches
 cnn

                                        our country is in genocide
                                        a word

                    I never thought   I'd use   in a poem

        why o lord   when we gifted
                                        you   our   medieval

                                        churches cut from a single rock   &
        the arc

                    the atlantic[12]   father   in heaven   my father's
                mother   country   is being
                                        destroyed
                                        lord you remember
                    lucy
                        we just need to know

        what you can   & cannot   fix
                                        do you know how easily lungs

                        can percuss
                                                how rage
                                can

                                        age & italicize

                                a body

        tell me you know   we arise

                from the same ancient   score
                                        the air

afro-heavy with

dandelions

getting ready to give up

their ghosts

tell us   is that where you are

VOX NOX

after self-care

real talk: how to   care

                                    for a self

evading

if it is possible   I can care while I evade my   self

    or is it that I   am too much   to care for

                                for even one life

      when I write I care   myself

          for a world though   I evade

am I getting   this right

      all I know

       is when I am depressed   I dirt

         devil the house   top to

                     bottom

      brush up my syntax

     pop vitamin d   but who in this house

   (or any)   figured out how   to become   hallowed

how long can you   go   evading
            the   broken

paraphernalia

   how long can you be

in the hold   of parts

     before they begin

        dispersing   evading into the lines

    you were meaning to say

          the word

               is what I do

to be in the hold   of   words   is hard

           but I will take it

      over the soft
           eterna

  thinking it's enough it's been
enough
   just   having

    thinking it's been enough

     just   having   a dream

VOX INFELIX / AGNOSIS

        my mind
           is at
                the funeral of oum   kalthoum
the tipping point   of lust

                how many suicides were decided
                there in the wailing flailing
                      orchestra
starved to   sad
          trombone
                death-parade
  I listen   to her

          suffering   is marrow is   the shroud

                of having loved
            & lost
love   a parade
unto death

     in case of emergency
     funeral   please keep   my books
ajar

                refrain   from parading
    the parts where I
        punctured

the starboard

of the ship to see   the leagues

                                        beneath my feet
        wanting to be remembered

                        enter   saltwater

                                                        enta   omri
                better   to be unloved

than loved   wrongly

        amirite   dear loves of old   may   you   live

                                forever   after
        on summer   & the opulence
                                of killing   time

                you & you & you

                                        washed even from the noumena
        the network I find myself

here   in the hood
        gardeners still   convene &

        converse in floral

glossa

green thumbs   flipping through

soil as story

lesson

for how to reach   spirit

not all roots are

permanent

a body can take root in many

places

even   post-wake

a tilling of a tomb you   see

[*let this be my will*

& testament]

that eyes seen what eyes always known

I may have no property

in my name   but in

my archival

corpus   whatever

remains is what remains

if not revolution

the yolk

of more to come

the corpus luteum   holds   the cavity of my anger

holds me   toward capital

strikes

a most courageous chord

me like midnight

or is it a gong

sounding through   all the years

from

autumn to june

done ~~made my m~~
undone
my mind

no one tells you

you can live

the life of the mind

& feel like no one

check it   butwhocaresnobigdealIwantmore

want more   breath

more   than   I   want   currency

or   are   they   the   same   thing

VOX EXEMPLUM

we are living in an im-

material world

who blessed this   technology

this destiny of   voiceprints[13]

did you   hear   designed to capture

all that   beauteous voice
you   had
when you were free

advanced

software to register
your register

how your words   "flow"

configure
into a digital   imprint

can't nobody   fake

I am trying to tell you   for the record

that so much   is on record

                                              best   hold   back
                                    your
                                         scream /

        best choose   carefully   who you leave
                                            a winded

                        voice mail for

    when the voice   converts to   an already-filed thing

            who holds the   master   recording

                              who   stores   the   wave-
                    form vibrations

                that swell & expel   mirror

                            soundwaves

                                all your own

                        you will hear seven voice samples
                        one of which may or may not be the person
                        responsible

    says the   theory of invariant speech

it may be useful to know

                                  the   main   strictures   of
                                  a speech
wave:

                time   frequency   & power

            or intensity

                    here lies the ghost

                            region   says the spectro-
graph

                             the samples will be played in
        random order

      say the specialists

          jaws & lips

                                check
dishevelled silhouette

       people raise their voices

with me when they know

          the physiological
   conditions involved

in freedom

I came for pleasure, not business

I long to say without fear

but trauma tricks you

say the behavioural theorists   I must   *check*

my vocal cords

may need to test the waters

testing testing

when all is said   & done   as earwitness

to recount is to relive

who will assist with this sound   *check*

you had to be there

to view how vital
signs grew scarce

to   *check*

my para-acoustic   pulse
check

police check
just want   to   *check*

to see how much   distortion

I can take

           in brasil   men who must
    resort to crime

        fill their mouths with cloth   *check*

        to mask their voices

   when they hold people up

          enough to make you gag

the way cashmoney is honey   & we killing

  the bees
        so many shootings in my hood

    won't nobody want to be
your neighbour

  people praying for cybertrucks

        check it
it a nobler religion I want

  all I have

    is this figure up in here
  my talk a trail

for the next   one   testing testing one

these words are   two   check

these words are   to voice

what content is

to form

but I am only

as good as the tidings

of   breath

allow

check   the logic of this interior   music   aria

must be   its sonic dialectic   of leaving   air

& the sinfonia

of return   of taking wing

using a kind

of soft   engineering

check it

I am only the messenger[14]

trying to chase that unchaste pitch

leaving behind   a chant or a song

a scat

& then some

[check it

this is a text

you won't hear the end of

check check

this is a test

I repeat

this is a test

testing testing]

AUTHOR'S NOTE

This collection borrows its title from a very specific musical analogy. On the standard pipe organ, the "vox humana" is a short-resonator reed stop so named because of its supposed resemblance to the human voice. As an amateur pianist, I have long been moved by the organ as an instrument, though I could never find the time/resources to learn how to play. Under the generous approval of former head organist at Trinity College (University of Toronto) John Tuttle, and during a time of great personal mourning, I was granted private access to the chapel organ, where I could conduct a music all my own (and unbeknownst to the largely white, largely male music-student body).

A portion of this manuscript was written and workshopped during my tenure as 2019–20 Barbara Smith Writer-in-Residence with Twelve Literary Arts (Cleveland, Ohio). This residency provided me with the time, space, and support to develop this manuscript in conjunction with a diverse range of creators and activists hailing from the Black Arts tradition. The culmination of my residency was an event entitled "In Her Word(s)," held at the St. John's Episcopal Church of Cleveland—a former stop on the Underground Railroad.

It was in this space that the enslaved hid and waited, en route to Canada, and where these poems were first performed.

Just as it was imperative for me to bring these poems to life in a site of living history, this book understands history as very much alive—and unwell, so long as bigotry and white supremacy continue to vex our world. Those with institutional positions of power can do good and open doors, but they often do not, finding it more suitable to silence voices, fracture subjectivities, police bodies. *Vox Humana* was written in the wake of George Floyd's murder and finalized in the midst of a global pandemic. This collection acknowledges all those who have passed unjustly. Their lives pass through us as echo, nudging us toward a more nuanced resistance.

The politics of *I can't breathe* has never been more relevant, as the world is running quite literally out of clean air. Yet we continue to speak up, demand a hearing. The use of slashes (/) in these poems, as opposed to traditional line breaks, convey breaks in thought and breath; the pauses in breath that make speech audible. Most of the poems are meant to be read/received in more than one way, as they contain more than one "voice." In turn, the "voice" in this book is multiple rather than universal, born from the particular set of experiences I have endured, as well as the search for a more healing frequency. This book is dedicated to all bodies and voices that are/have been compromised in some way. And to my father, who has always inspired me to call out those in violation of human rights and continue doing the solemn (breath) work of keeping (Black) voice and (African) oral history alive.

ACKNOWLEDGEMENTS

Thank you first and foremost to the team at Book*hug, with a special thanks to Hazel and Jay Millar for their support, kindness, and invaluable feedback every step of the way, and to my editor, the wondrous Shazia Hafiz Ramji, for truly hearing me/this book out.

Thank you to *Columbia Journal*, *The Fiddlehead*, *The Puritan*, and *Boston Review*, where these poems appeared in earlier manifestations.

Thanks to the Canada Council for the Arts, Ontario Arts Council, and Toronto Arts Council for helping fund the completion of this book.

A heartfelt thanks to Daniel Grey-Kontar and the family at Twelve Literary Arts in Cleveland for hosting me as the 2019–20 Barbara Smith Writer-in-Residence, and to Rev. Noah Sutterisch for helping coordinate my final reading at St. John's Episcopal Church, aka "Station Hope," a former stop on the Underground Railroad. My time in "The Land" will not be forgotten.

To the poets/creators whose words helped me breathe this book into life and continue to inspire me ad infinitum: M. NourbeSe Philip, Wayde Compton, Lillian Allen, Olive Senior, Kaie Kellough, Liz Howard, Canisia Lubrin—I hold you in the highest regard.

To poet and sister supreme Sonia Sanchez for believing in and blessing my work with your eyes/wisdom/love—all I have is praise, forever.

Finally, to my family and friends near and far, loved ones both here/present and ancestral/effervescent, who kept listening to me ramble, kept insisting with me that poetry matters—thank you, from my heart: it means the world.

NOTES

1. This definition, along with the definitions that appear on pages 13, 47, and 104, are all adapted from the Online Etymology Dictionary (etymonline.com).

2 Using tomography, scientists reproduced the voice of an ancient Egyptian priest by creating a 3-D-printed replica of his mummified vocal tract. The outside of the mummy's coffin reads "Nesyamun, true of voice."

3 From the Greek words meaning "without speech," a condition characterized by reduced speech output or impairment in thinking that affects language abilities. It can involve using fewer words or answering only what is directly asked and/or speaking in a way that may be vague, repetitive, or overly concrete. While largely associated with schizophrenia, dementia, and severe depression, alogia can also be a secondary effect, resulting from primary symptoms (e.g., psychosis or anxiety).

4 In the early afternoon of May 29, 2019, Arnav Gupta of Bethesda, Maryland, set himself on fire in front of sightseers at Ellipse Park in downtown Washington, DC, steps from the White House; he died from his injuries.

5 On October 2, 1937, Rafael Trujillo (1891–1961), dictator of the Dominican Republic, ordered 20,000 Black people killed because they could not pronounce the letter "r" in *perejil*, the Spanish word for parsley.

6 Located in the windchest of the pipe organ, a pallet is the part of the pipe used to open and close holes that admit air into the pipe, causing its mouth to "speak" when the key is depressed.

7 A euphemistic term c. 1930. To fare-ill, rather than fare-well.

8 The asterisk (*), from the Late Latin *asteriscus*, or "little star," is a typographical symbol or glyph that resembles a conventional image of a star, commonly used to call out a footnote, censor offensive words, indicate a correction to a previous message, or emphasize a particular part of text (often linked to a marginal comment).

9 *Transpire* (v.) 1590s, "pass off in the form of a vapour or liquid," from French *transpirer* (16c.), from Latin *trans* "across, beyond; through" (see trans-) + *spirare* "to breathe" (see spirit (n.)). To "leak out, become known" is recorded from 1741. Erroneous meaning "take place, happen" is almost as old, first recorded in 1755.

10 The PIE (a 6,000-year-old Proto-Indo-European language) word for earth, or "from the soil" (origin of the later Latin terms *homo, humanus, humus*).

11 "To pull out all the stops" originally refers to the stop knobs on a pipe organ, used to regulate the instrument's sound by selecting which sets of pipes are active at a given time. Each pipe plays a note, and the pipes are arranged in sets (called ranks) according to type and quality of sound.

12 Formerly known as the Ethiopian Sea.

13 Voiceprints ("sound spectrograms") are visual representations of the frequencies and amplitude of sounds as represented on a timeline. In a forensic setting, spectrographic analysis involves visual comparison of the spectrogram-questioned voice with one from a known voice, typically the voice of the defendant in a criminal trial. Most of those who conduct this kind of analysis are not phoneticians, but rather police officers and technicians who have been trained for this specific task and typically have limited backgrounds in acoustics/phonetics.

14 In the case of human bodily death, hearing is the last sense to go.

1

ABOUT THE AUTHOR

Adebe DeRango-Adem is a writer and former
attendee of the Jack Kerouac School of
Disembodied Poetics (Naropa University),
where she mentored with poets Anne Waldman
and Amiri Baraka. She is the author of three
previous full-length poetry books: *Ex Nihilo*,
a finalist for the Dylan Thomas Prize; *Terra
Incognita*, nominated for the Pat Lowther
Memorial Award; and *The Unmooring*.
A poem from *The Unmooring* was featured
in the 2019 *Poem In Your Pocket* anthology,
co-created by the League of Canadian Poets
and the Academy of American Poets. DeRango-
Adem served as the 2019–20 Barbara Smith
Writer-in-Residence with Twelve Literary
Arts, in Cleveland, Ohio. Her poem, "Genus /
Provectus," won the 2021 *Boston Review* Annual
Poetry Contest. She lives in Toronto.

PHOTO: SELENA PHILLIPS-BOYLE

COLOPHON

Manufactured as the first edition of
Vox Humana
in the fall of 2022 by Book*hug Press

Edited for the press by Shazia Hafiz Ramji
Copy-edited by Stuart Ross
Proofread by Charlene Chow
Design and typesetting by Gareth Lind, Lind Design
Cover image: KRONA/Shutterstock.com
Inside front and back cover image: iStock / Alex Potemkin
Type: Mundo Serif and Mark

Printed in Canada

bookhugpress.ca